LITTLE QUICK FIX:

SEE NUMBERS IN DATA

#LittleQuickFix

Sara Miller McCune founded SAGE Publishing in 1965 to support the dissemination of usable knowledge and educate a global community. SAGE publishes more than 1000 journals and over 800 new books each year, spanning a wide range of subject areas. Our growing selection of library products includes archives, data, case studies and video. SAGE remains majority owned by our founder and after her lifetime will become owned by a charitable trust that secures the company's continued independence.

Los Angeles | London | New Delhi | Singapore | Washington DC | Melbourne

SEE NUMBERS IN DATA

John MacInnes

Los Angeles | London | New Delhi
Singapore | Washington DC | Melbourne

Los Angeles | London | New Delhi
Singapore | Washington DC | Melbourne

SAGE Publications Ltd
1 Oliver's Yard
55 City Road
London EC1Y 1SP

SAGE Publications Inc.
2455 Teller Road
Thousand Oaks, California 91320

SAGE Publications India Pvt Ltd
B 1/I 1 Mohan Cooperative Industrial Area
Mathura Road
New Delhi 110 044

SAGE Publications Asia-Pacific Pte Ltd
3 Church Street
#10-04 Samsung Hub
Singapore 049483

Editor: Aly Owen
Production editor: Ian Antcliff
Marketing manager: Ben Griffin-Sherwood
Design: Shaun Mercier
Typeset by: C&M Digitals (P) Ltd, Chennai, India
Printed in the UK

First published 2019

Library of Congress Control Number: 2018962989

British Library Cataloguing in Publication data

A catalogue record for this book is available from the British Library

ISBN 978-1-5264-6679-2

Contents

Everything in this book!

Section 1 **Why is most data numerical data?** Numerical data is everywhere! We need numbers to help us describe things with detail and precision.

Section 2 **What is the average, level or central tendency of data?** The average for some data is the simplest summary available of any data, whether it is your income or the number of stars in a galaxy. It tells you about the size of the typical observations in a set of data.

Section 3 **What is the spread or dispersion of data?** The spread of data concerns whether the data clusters round the average or if the data is more spread out. Finding the spread means we can better understand the variation in our data.

Section 4 How do I understand the data in a graph? Pictures are often better than numbers to describe data. While sizes, shapes and patterns can be intuitive, three questions make understanding any graph easier.

Section 5 What are the five main kinds of graph? Distinguishing different types of graph will help you better understand the numerical data they communicate. Bar charts, histograms, box plots, scatterplots and line charts are the most common types of graph you will encounter.

Section 6 What is scientific notation? Powers and scientific notation allow us to express very small or large numbers without resorting to endless zeroes.

Section 7 How can I use and interpret numbers in data well? Like anything else, numerical data can be used well or badly. Follow these seven simple rules to use and interpret numerical data well.

Describe things with detail and precision

Section 1

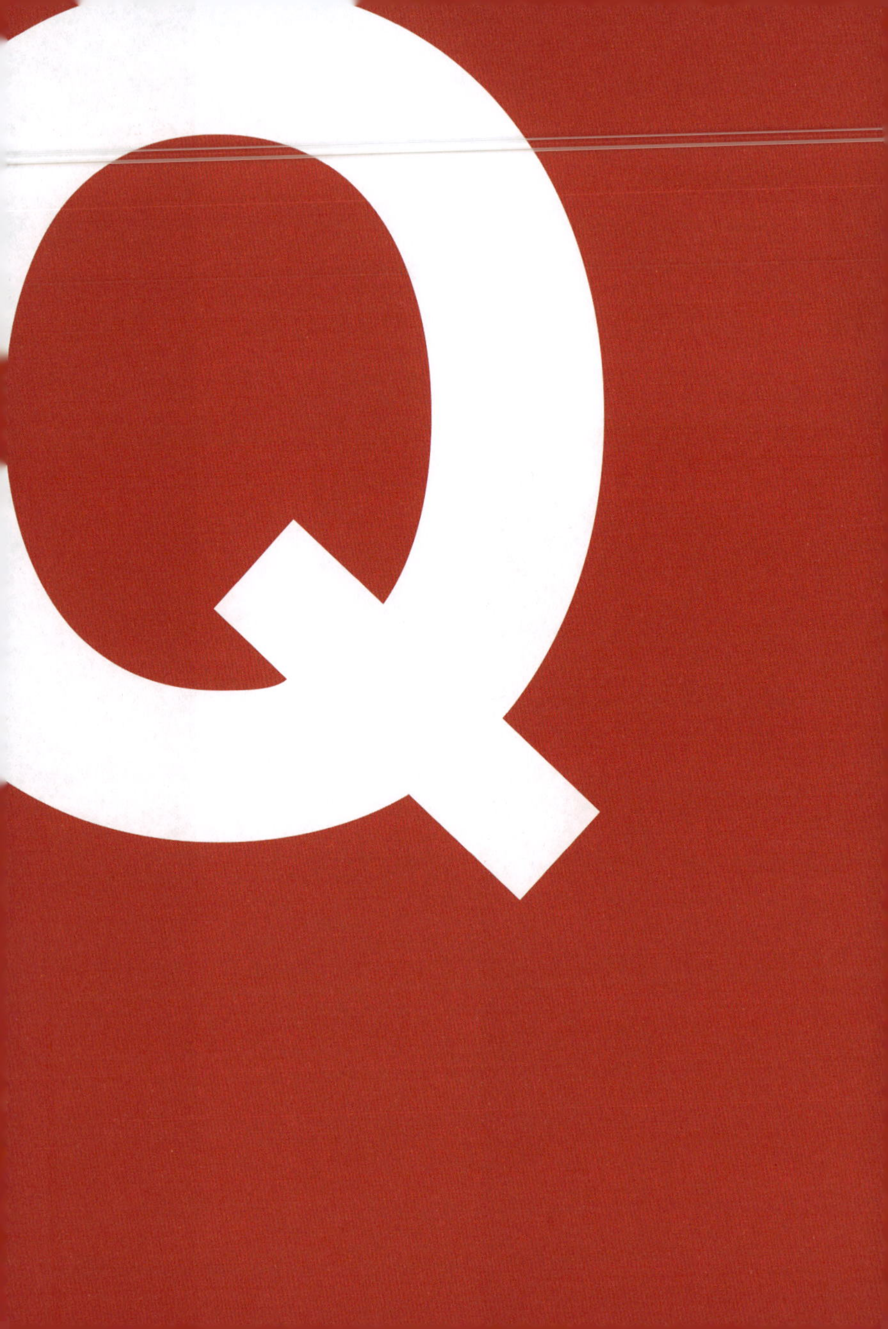
Q

Why is most data numerical data?

Only numbers give us the detail or precision we need to describe things well.

Data means numbers

Data is a description of a collection of things or people. Whenever we want to describe many examples of the same or similar things, numbers are the only option. Digital technology, from calculators to the internet, all run on numerical code.

This has made the capture of information about organizations and people easier than before, generating ever-increasing amounts of data.

But just like any other kind of information, numerical data can be excellent or poor quality, and can be used well or badly.

WHAT WE MEAN WHEN WE TALK ABOUT DATA

Data is always **a description of some collection of things or people**. You will find many different terms used both for the description and for the collection. Sometimes the description is given a name directly, like 'income', 'ethnicity', 'population size', and sometimes it is referred to as a variable with values. The individual objects or people described may be called observations or cases, or referred to collectively as a sample or population. Putting both together we get a data series, data points or just 'data'. Such language is not always used consistently and clearly, so to avoid any confusion in this book we follow these rules:

- **case** is the object or person that is measured (e.g. an adult in the USA)
- **variable** is the feature that is measured about them (e.g. how they voted in the 2016 US presidential election)
- **observation** is the result of that measurement (e.g. voted Clinton)
- **values** describe the range these results can take (e.g. Clinton, Trump, Other, Did not vote)

Numbers help us measure

Data, mostly in numerical form, is now vital to almost every aspect of the modern world, and that includes every university discipline and all the social sciences.

Most data is numerical because only **numbers give us a consistent sense of scale or volume**. Expressions like 'most', 'some' or 'a few' are often just too vague. When we can measure things, whether it is the behaviour or norms of individuals, or the characteristics of organizations or institutions, we can understand them better.

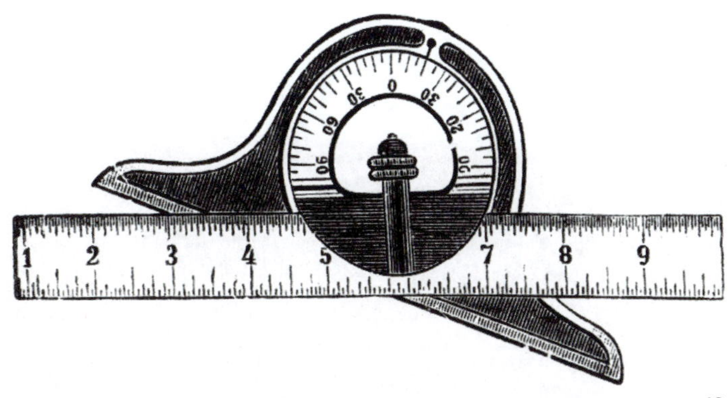

Numbers help us describe detail

Numbers are the only way of capturing and processing information at scale. If we have two or three examples of something to describe, we can use all the subtlety and colour of language. But if we have two or three dozen, let alone 2 or 3 million, we can only cope by classifying and measuring using numbers.

Numbers are straightforward

Numerical data can appear intimidating, especially if it has been a while since you did maths or worked with numbers. Like any other skill, dealing with numbers is something that gets rusty and clunky if you have not used it. The good news is that you need only a few straightforward skills to deal with most data – no calculus, trigonometry or quadratic equations, mostly just arithmetic. Even better news is that **these skills are useful for all kinds of other life skills as well**, from distinguishing reliable news from fake nonsense, to working out the real cost of an internet deal.

TRUE/FALSE

Tick the statements that are true

- ☐ Numbers provide vague information
- ☐ Numbers give us detail and precision
- ☐ Numbers give us a consistent sense of scale
- ☐ Numbers help us capture information about people and organizations

Statements 2, 3 and 4 are all true.

Answers

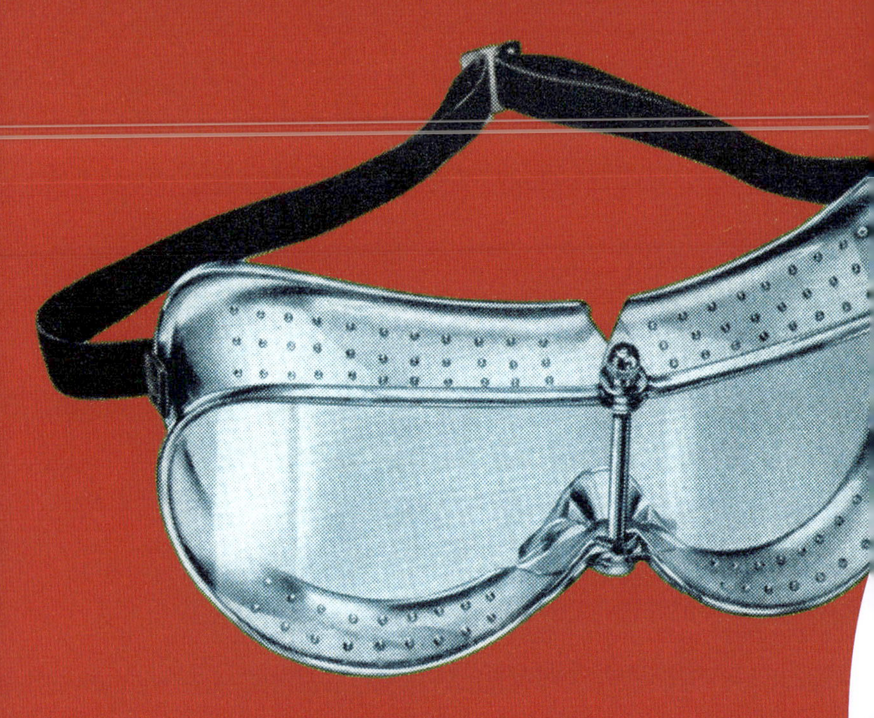

The average is the simplest summary available

Section 2

What is the average, level or central tendency of data?

The average (also known as level or central tendency) tells us about the size of the typical values of observations in a particular set of data.

Size matters

Often we have numerical measurements on a large group. Listing the income or ethnic group of 1000 people would give us a mass of indigestible data. We summarize large amounts of data by producing a typical, or average, measurement, also known as the level or central tendency.

The *mean* and the *median* are two ways of describing the average, central tendency or level of data. The arithmetic *mean* is an average created by summing all the observations and dividing by the number of cases. The *median* is an average created by ranking all observations and taking the value of the middle observation.

DEFINING AVERAGE

Usually the first thing we want to know about anything is how big it is.

- Is this flu outbreak a budding pandemic, or just a few extra cases?
- Do people here earn $10 an hour, or $100 or $1000?
- Does almost everyone, a lot of people or just about no one do or think something?

The *average*, also called the *level* or *central tendency*, gives us a **typical value that summarizes all our cases and gives an indication of how big or small the values in the data are**.

There are two useful averages: the mean and the median.

Measure of average 1: the mean

The *mean* is **calculated by summing all our observations and dividing by the number of cases.**

Consider height. Describing height to a visiting Martian, I could say the mean, or average, height of women is 170cm. For men it is around 180cm. Nobody is 17cm or 17m tall.

Of course this does not mean every man or woman is of average height. Nor is every man taller than every woman. However, in only a couple of numbers I have summarized the heights of about 5 billion individuals.

The impact of outliers

The mean works well as an average for height because there are very few extremely tall or extremely short people. **The greater the distance of any individual observation from the mean, the greater is its impact on it.** Cases with values that are very different to most of the others in a series are known as *outliers*. They often indicate that something unusual is going on.

Measure of average 2: the median

Data on workers' weekly pay shows that in the UK in 2017 the mean was £443. That figure is produced by totalling the pay of every worker and dividing by the number of workers.

However, another figure for average weekly pay is the *median*.

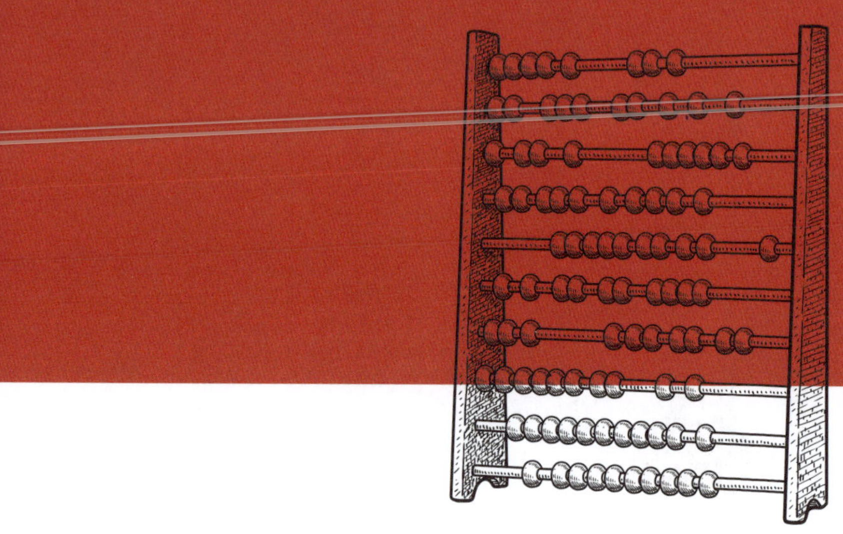

To calculate a median we **rank all the cases in order from the lowest to the highest observation, and select the middle case**, halfway up the ranking. If we have an odd number of cases, there is only one case in the middle. If we have an even number of cases we take the mean of the middle two cases.

When we rank workers according to their weekly pay, from the lowest to the highest, £415 is the pay of the worker exactly halfway up this ranking.

The median is not impacted by outliers

Cases with very small or very large values have no more impact on the median than any others, because such values do not affect the ranking of cases.

A small number of workers have very high earnings. This raises the mean, so that far more than half of all workers have pay *below* this average. The median splits the workforce exactly in half.

CALCULATING MEANS AND MEDIANS

I recorded the units of alcohol I drank for the last two weeks. Grab a calculator and work out the mean and median amount. What do these tell you about my drinking habits?

1 0 0 3 0 9 11 0 0 2 2 0 8 6

Sum of all the values:

....

Number of cases:

....

The mean:

....

CHECKPOINT

Order of values from lowest to highest:

....

Rank of values from lowest to highest:

....

The median:

....

So, what can you say about my drinking habits?

....

....

ANSWERS

Sum of all the values = 42

Number of cases = 14

The mean: $42 \div 14 = 3$

CHECKPOINT

Ordered observations:

						Median							
1	2	3	4	5	6	7	8	9	10	11	12	13	14
0	0	0	0	0	0	1	2	2	3	6	8	9	11

Median = (1 + 2) ÷ 2 = 1.5

Drinking habits: Most days I don't drink anything at all, but on some days (weekends?) I drink a lot. My median intake is less than 2 units, but my weekend benders push the mean up to 3 units.

Section

Finding the spread means we can better understand variation

3

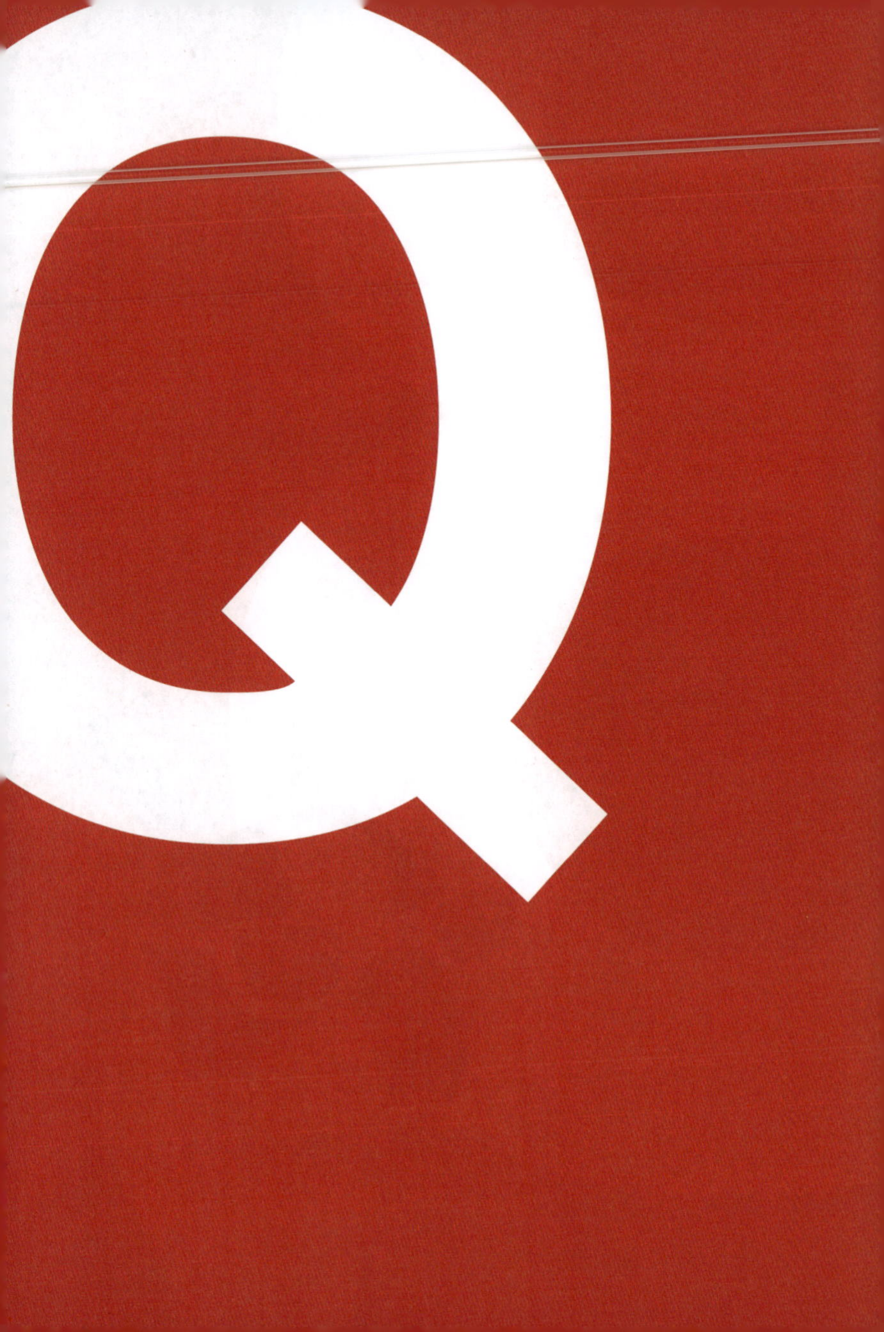

What is the spread or dispersion of data?

The spread (also known as dispersion) describes whether observations are clustered closely together or spread apart.

Mind the gap

Means or medians tell us about 'typical' values for the data we have. But how typical is typical?

Perhaps all the data values are very close to the values for the mean or the median. But they might also be spread out so much that most values are far from the average, and few are actually anywhere near it.

The *standard deviation* and the *interquartile range* (IQR) are two ways to measure the spread or dispersion of data around the mean or median. We may also be interested in outliers (or extreme values), which are values that are very different to the others.

DESCRIBING VARIATION IN DATA

Some data contains more variation than other data. Think about the incomes and heights discussed in the previous section. Few people are more than about 30cm shorter or taller than the average height. In contrast, some people earn only a fraction of median income, while a few earn many times that amount.

The *spread* or *dispersion* of the data measures whether observations are clustered together near the average (like height) or vary more widely (like income).

Just as there are two averages, the mean and median, there are **two corresponding measures of spread: the *standard deviation* and the *interquartile range*.**

MEASURE OF SPREAD 1: STANDARD DEVIATION

The standard deviation **measures how far from the mean value most observations are located**.

To calculate the standard deviation, we can use the example of weekly pay.

FYI: *You should never have to carry out the next series of calculations by hand. Statistical software, any spreadsheet package or a calculator will do it for you!*

CALCULATING THE STANDARD DEVIATION

Step 1

Subtract each observation from the mean (£443) to get a *residual* figure.

If someone earned £500, the residual would be 500 − 443 = +£57

If someone earned £250, it would be 250 − 443 = −£193

If we summed all the residuals, we would always get zero (which by definition must be the average distance of all observations from the average for them all).

Step 2

To avoid this, *square* them. Since a negative number multiplied by another negative number is a positive number, squaring residuals makes all our numbers positive.

Step 3

Next, total these squared residuals, and divide by the number of cases.

Step 4

To undo the effect of squaring, we take the square root of this figure and arrive at the standard deviation.

The standard deviation for weekly pay works out at £233.

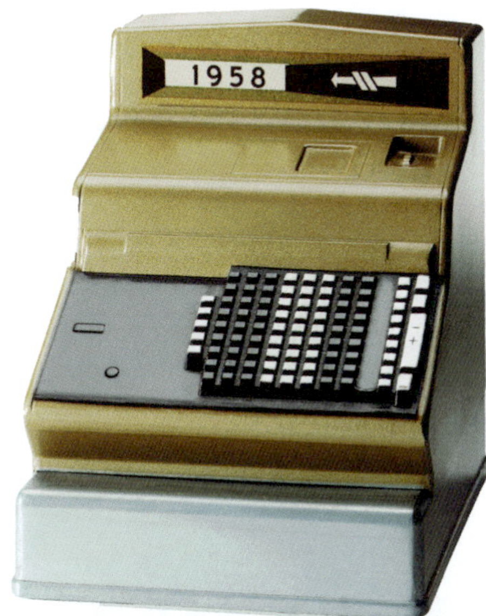

MOST OBSERVATIONS ARE WITHIN ONE STANDARD DEVIATION

A useful rule of thumb for most data is that **a majority of the observations are found within roughly one standard deviation of the mean** and most (over 90%) observations lie within about two standard deviations.

For our pay data, this means we would expect most people to be paid between

mean – one standard deviation → 443 - 233 = £210

mean + one standard deviation → 443 + 233 = £676

And we would expect nearly everyone to get paid between

443 - 2 × (233) → 443 - 466 = -£23

443 + 2 × (233) → 443 + 466 = £909

The figure of –£23 is a reminder that this is a rough rule of thumb. Nobody is paid negative wages! However, we would expect few people to earn over £900 each week.

THE BIGGER THE VARIATION, THE HIGHER THE STANDARD DEVIATION

If everyone in the UK earned much the same, just as they had much the same height, the standard deviation of gross weekly income might be only a few pounds. Because incomes vary dramatically, the standard deviation is much higher.

MEASURE OF SPREAD 2: INTERQUARTILE RANGE

Just as the median is the value that is ranked halfway up all values, so the *quartiles* are the values ranked halfway from the lowest value to the median (the *lower* quartile) and halfway from the median to the highest value (the *upper* quartile).

The distance between the lower and upper quartile is called the *interquartile range* (IQR) and covers the middle 50% of cases. For our weekly pay data it would be

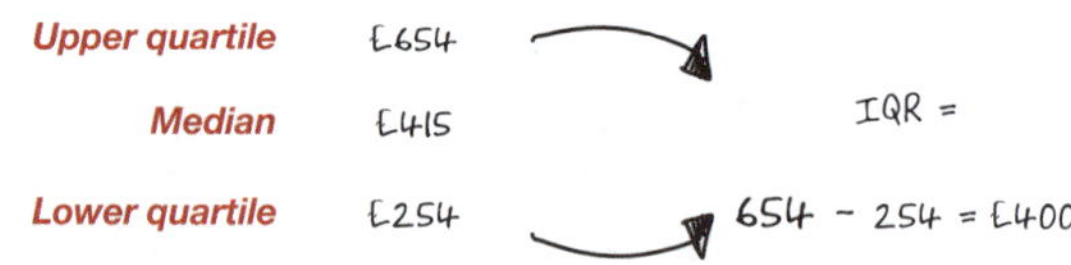

UNDERSTANDING QUINTILES, DECILES AND PERCENTILES

In the same way that quartiles describe the data points found in each quarter of the way up the ranking of all data points

- quintiles divide them into five equal parts
- deciles into ten equal parts
- percentiles into a hundred equal parts

Thus the first quintile would be 20% of the way up the ranking, the first decile 10%, and the first percentile 1%.

THE IMPORTANCE OF OUTLIERS AND EXTREME VALUES

Sometimes one or more observations take a value far below or above the others. As we saw in Section 2, these observations are called outliers, or extreme values. Usually they need special attention. **Understanding why an observation is so different to the others is often important.** It might be the result of an error.

HOW TO CALCULATE THE INTERQUARTILE RANGE

Table 1 shows the percentage of people in 21 countries in the World Values survey who said that religion was very important to them in their everyday lives.

Country	Per cent
Argentina	24
Belarus	16
Brazil	52
Chile	24
China	3
Egypt	94
Germany	13
Hong Kong	12
India	67
Iraq	85
Japan	5
Nigeria	90
Pakistan	90
Philippines	86
Russia	14
Singapore	43
South Africa	56
South Korea	26
Sweden	8
Ukraine	26
USA	40

DO IT YOURSELF

Step 1

Rank the observations from the lowest to the highest percentage, by filling in the blank cells in the table.

Country	Rank	%
	21	
	20	
	19	
	18	
	17	
	16	
	15	
	14	
	13	
	12	
	11	
	10	
	9	
	8	
	7	
	6	
	5	
	4	
	3	
	2	
	1	

IQR = 67 − 14 = 53

Answers

Step 2

Use the rankings to work out the minimum, the median, the lower and upper quartiles, the interquartile range and the maximum for this data.

Minimum: ....

Lower quartile: ....

Median: ....

Upper quartile: ....

Maximum: ....

Step 3

Based on these quartiles, what is your interquartile range?

Upper quartile ____ – Lower quartile _____ = Interquartile range _____

Check your answers on the next page!

ANSWERS

Country	Rank	%	
Egypt	21	94	Maximum
Nigeria	20	90	
Pakistan	19	90	
Philippines	18	86	
Iraq	17	85	
India	16	67	Upper quartile
South Africa	15	56	
Brazil	14	52	
Singapore	13	43	
USA	12	40	
Ukraine	11	26	Median
South Korea	10	26	
Argentina	9	24	
Chile	8	24	
Belarus	7	16	
Russia	6	14	Lower quartile
Germany	5	13	
Hong Kong	4	12	
Sweden	3	8	
Japan	2	5	
China	1	3	Minimum

Got it?

Q: What two ways can we use to measure the dispersion of our data?

Got it!

A: Standard deviation and interquartile range.

Three questions make understanding any graph easier

4

Section

Q

How do I understand the data in a graph?

Answering three questions about any graph, chart or plot is key to understanding what it shows.

How do graphs work?

All graphics work by making area or length proportional to numbers in the data, but they can do this in many different ways, which may make them confusing. They may display the original data, or summaries of that data, like the values of the mean or quartiles.

To make sense of any graph, we first have to work out what it displays by looking at its title and asking three questions about what variables the graph covers, how the data varies, and whether the graph displays original data or a summary of it.

THE BASIC ANATOMY OF A GRAPH

All graphs are laid out on two 'axes', the horizontal or X-axis and the vertical or Y-axis.

The title of the graph, together with a description of each of its two axes, should contain the information needed to understand its contents. Sometimes graphs contain a *legend*: that is, a text box that explains any colour coding in the graph. Read these carefully!

Interpreting the anatomy

Figure 1 shows the changing price of light over the last 700 years. Once you see that the horizontal axis plots years, a glance at the graph quickly reveals one reason for the term 'the Dark Ages': until the end of the nineteenth century, light was vastly more costly than it is today. A closer look at the vertical axis reveals much more detail. The prices are in year 2000 equivalent British pounds, to adjust for inflation, and the price for one hour of the equivalent light output to a 100 watt incandescent bulb is shown. Note also the text box providing the data source of the graph. **Be sceptical of graphics that do not clearly specify the original data on which they are based.**

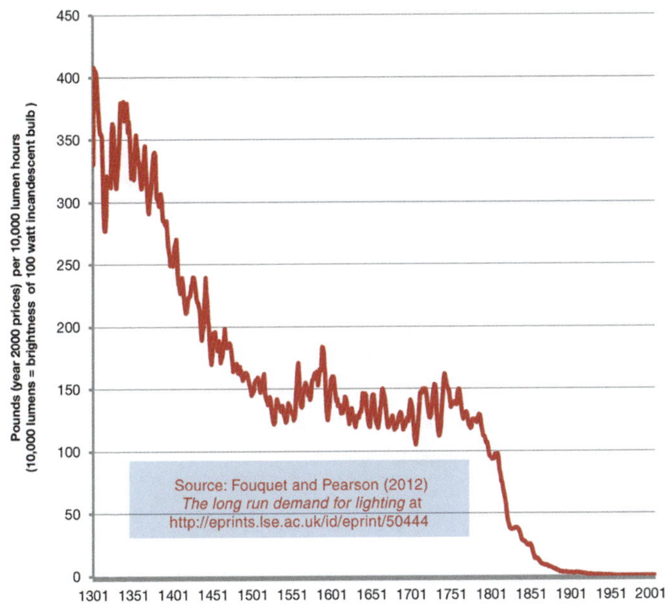

Figure 1 The price of light, 1301 to 2001

Source: Fouquet and Pearson (2012) *The long run demand for lighting* at http://eprints.lse.ac.uk/id/eprint/50444

To understand a graph and what it displays, ask yourself the following three questions

Question 1 Does the graph cover only one variable, or more than one?

Some graphs summarize only one variable or data series, like **Figure 1**. We see the changing values on the vertical axis as we move through time on the horizontal axis. More often, graphs present information on one variable, broken down by different values for one or more other variables.

Figure 2 shows the number of people in the world without access to improved sanitation, broken down by world region, over the last 25 years. The legend to the right of the graph shows which colour represents each world region.

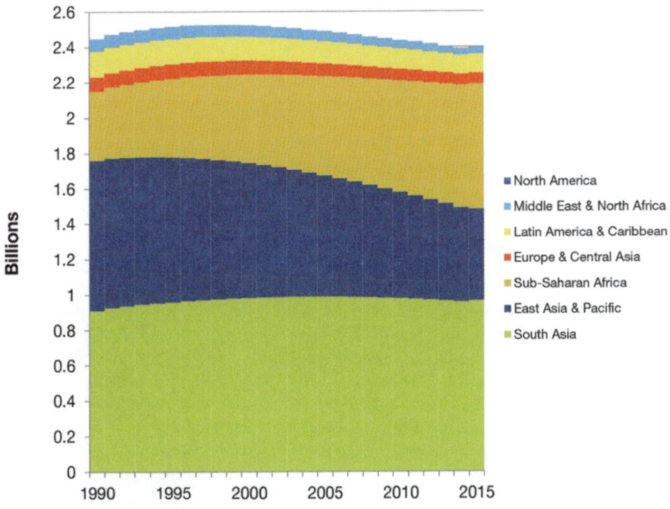

Figure 2 People without access to improved sanitation by world region, 1990 to 2015

Question 2 Does the data vary continuously, in the form of a number or quantity, or is it divided up into categories with labels?

The cost of light in **Figure 1** is something that varies continuously, taking any value from hundreds of pounds to fractions of a penny. **Figure 2** shows an example of both kinds of variation. The number of people varies continuously, while the regions of the world are a list of categories.

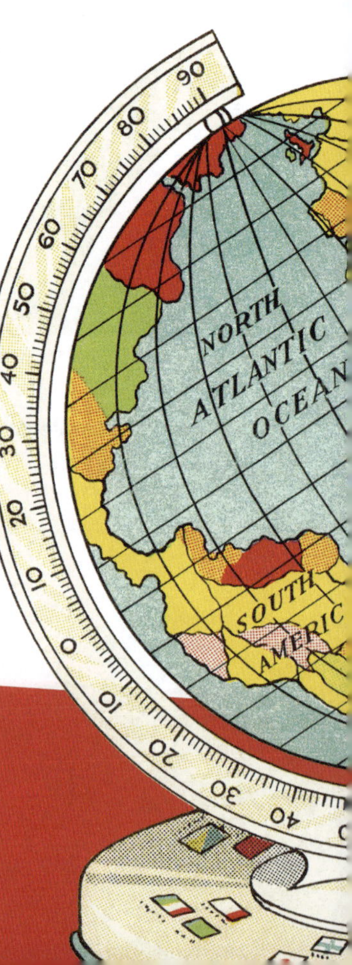

Question 3 Is the data represented in the graph the original data or a summary of it?

The data presented in **Figure 1** is an estimate of the average cost of light gleaned from historical records, so it is a summary of data.
Figure 2 presents the original data. The entire world population has been allocated into regions and then divided into two groups: those with and those without access to improved sanitation.

YOUR GRAPH INTERPRETATION CHECKLIST

Have you determined...

- [ ] The title and axes of the graph?
- [ ] If the graph displays one or more than one variable?
- [ ] If the variables are continuous or a series of categories?
- [ ] If the graph reports the original data or a summary of it?

CHECKPOINT

Section 5

Distinguishing between graph types will help you understand the data they communicate

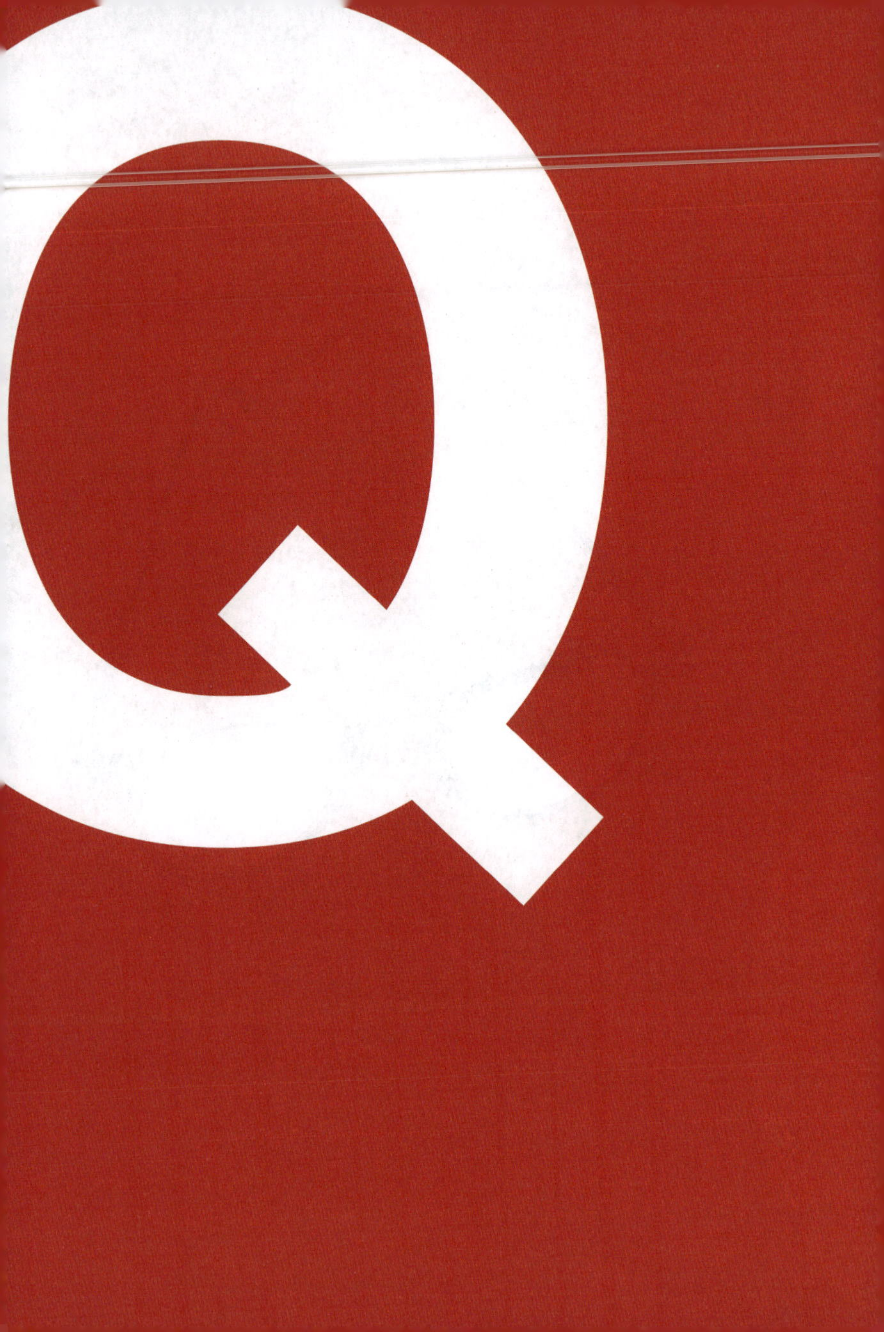

What are the five main kinds of graph?

The five most common types of graph you will likely encounter are bar charts, histograms, box plots, scatterplots and line charts.

Distinguishing different types of graph

In order to understand what a graph is telling you and what it says about the data it is communicating, it is important to be able to distinguish different kinds of graph. There are five main types:

1 **Bar charts** display continuous data by the categories of a variable

2 **Histograms** display all the data for one variable that varies continuously

3 **Box plots** display summary data for one variable that varies continuously

4 **Scatterplots** display two variables that vary continuously

5 **Line charts** display summary data for one or more variables by period of time

WHAT IS A BAR CHART?

In bar charts, the *height* or *length* of **a bar corresponds to the number or proportion of observations that fit into each category of a variable**, or to some summary data about each category of that variable. Because bar charts are so versatile, you need to decipher just what they show.

Figure 3 describes the results of an August 2016 poll for the US presidential election.

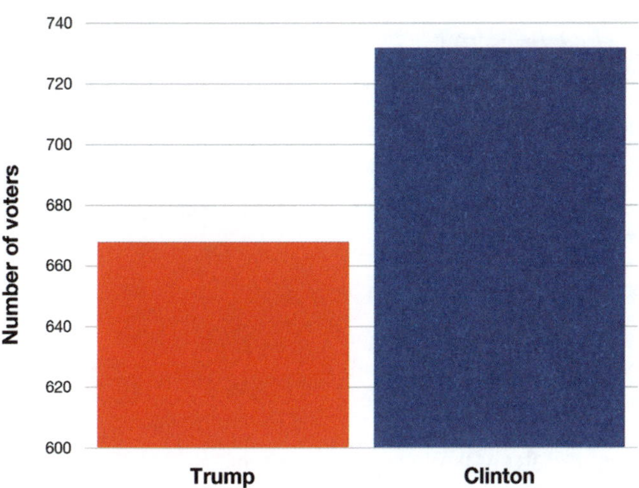

Figure 3 Voting intention, 2016

CHECKPOINT

Using the three questions to understand a bar chart

To understand Figure 3, ask the three questions we discussed in Section 4.

1 What is displayed on each axis?

Vertical axis: ....

Horizontal axis: ....

2 Does each axis show continuous variation or categories?

Vertical: ....

Horizontal: ....

3 Does the graph show original data or summaries of it?

....

Answers

1 Vertical axis: number of observations for a variable about voting intention
Horizontal axis: each category of the variable (Clinton, Trump)

2 Vertical axis: continuous variation
Horizontal axis: categories

3 Original data

Getting your head around bar chart data

This bar chart displays the original data for one variable, with the height of the bars above each category of the variable showing the number of observations taking that value.

Note that the vertical axis of the graph starts at 600, not zero. This makes it easier to see accurately how many observations are in each category, but it also magnifies the difference between them. Clinton's support was not double that for Trump.

Getting your head around clustered bar charts

Figure 4 shows a *clustered* bar chart. As before, **it shows the original data, but now it breaks this down by a second variable:** the ethnicity of the voters who were polled. Because, like voting intention, this variable takes the form of categories, it can be displayed along the horizontal axis as well. To distinguish the two variables, different colours are used to represent support for Trump and Clinton within each ethnicity category. Because bars can be placed side by side they make comparisons easy.

Bar charts are not always vertical

The bars in a bar chart can be either vertical or horizontal, but one of the axes of a bar chart *always* displays the categories of one or more variables represented by the bars, while the bars themselves always represent either the number or proportions of the original data observations, or some summary measure of them.

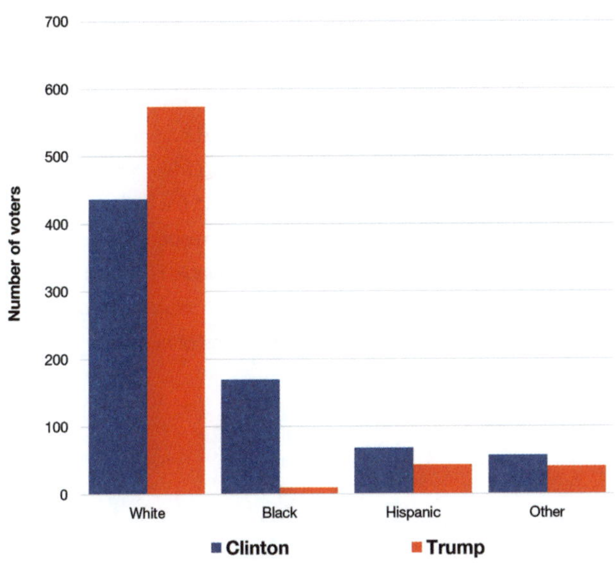

Figure 4 **Voting intention by ethnicity, 2016**

Source: ONS

WHAT IS A HISTOGRAM?

Unlike bar charts, **histograms are only used for data where there is a *continuous* range of values, rather than categories**. Histograms display the range of values taken by the data along the horizontal axis and the number or proportion of observations corresponding to each value along the vertical axis. Usually *only one* variable is shown in a histogram. Histograms can be used to show more information on the shape of distributions without the need for dozens of numbers.

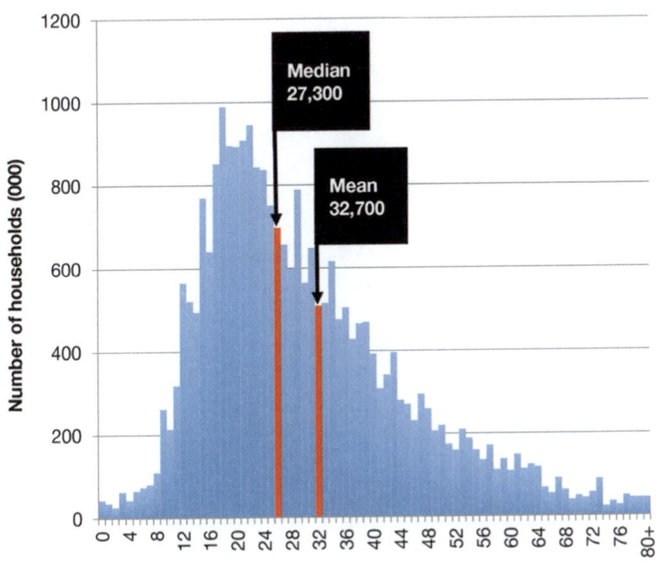

Figure 5 Annual equivalized household income (£000s)

CHECKPOINT

Using the three questions to understand a histogram

Examine Figure 5 and ask our three questions.

1 What is displayed on each axis?

Vertical axis: ....

Horizontal axis: ....

2 Does each axis show continuous variation or categories?

Vertical: ....

Horizontal: ....

3 Does the graph show original data or summaries of it?

....

Answers

1 Vertical axis: number of observations (households)
Horizontal axis: income in £1000 bands

2 Vertical: continuous variation
Horizontal: continuous

3 Original data

Histogram bars do not have to be the same width

It is the *area* above any range of values that matters in a histogram. At the bottom right of Figure 5 the last bar represents *all* the incomes above £80,000. If the axis continued in £1000 increments it would be much longer. However, we can 'squash' these final bars into a narrower bar that also becomes higher because it now represents all households with these higher incomes.

WHAT IS A BOX PLOT?

Like histograms, box plots describe a single variable that varies continuously. Instead of showing the whole range of values, **box plots display the upper and lower quartiles as a box, with a line through it showing the median.** Whiskers in the form of a 'T' extending from the top and bottom of the box cover where most data values lie.

Just like bar charts, box plots can be clustered to make comparisons easy. **Figure 6** shows the distribution of normal weekly working hours for men (in blue) and women (in green) in three countries. Just by looking at the position of the boxes, we can tell a lot about the situation without even looking at the numbers.

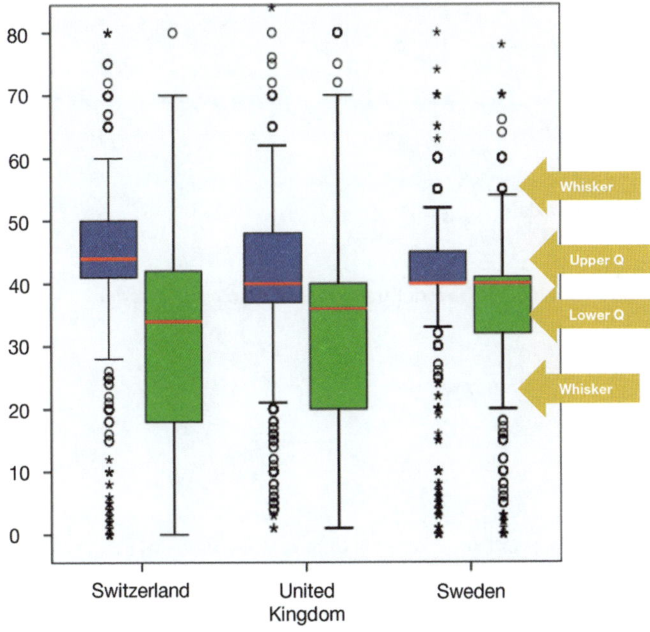

Figure 6 **Normal weekly working hours in three countries**

Source: ESS

CHECKPOINT

Using the three questions to understand a box plot

Examine Figure 6 and ask our three questions.

1 What is displayed on each axis?

Vertical axis: ....

Horizontal axis: ....

2 Does each axis show continuous variation or categories?

Vertical: ....

Horizontal: ....

3 Does the graph show original data or summaries of it?

....

Answers

1 Vertical axis: number of hours worked
Horizontal axis: men and women by country

2 Vertical: continuous variation
Horizontal: categories

3 Original data

WHAT IS A SCATTERPLOT?

A scatterplot **always displays the original data for two variables that vary continuously for the same set of cases.** Each data point on the plot represents the combination of two values for each case. **Figure 7** shows average UK winter rainfall for the last 250 years. The two variables are *rainfall* and *year*. Each data point represents the rainfall (in inches on the vertical axis) for each year (shown on the horizontal axis). Again, without looking at the numbers we can see that the amount of rain varies dramatically from year to year with little apparent trend over time.

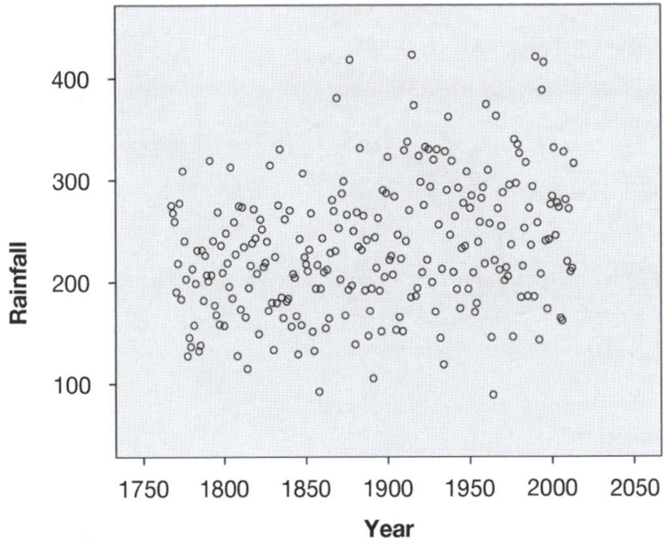

Figure 7 UK rainfall in inches (December to February)

Source: metoffice.gov.uk

CHECKPOINT

Using the three questions to understand a scatterplot

Examine Figure 7 and ask our three questions.

1 What is displayed on each axis?

Vertical axis: ....

Horizontal axis: ....

2 Does each axis show continuous variation or categories?

Vertical: ....

Horizontal: ....

3 Does the graph show original data or summaries of it?

....

Answers

1 Vertical axis: amount of rainfall in inches
Horizontal axis: year

2 Vertical: continuous variation
Horizontal: continuous variation

3 Summary data

#LittleQuickFix

WHAT IS A LINE CHART?

Line charts are **good for displaying trends over time**. They are exactly the same as scatterplots, except that the coordinates are joined by a line. They work only if there is not too much variation from one time period to the next (imagine a line connecting all the coordinates on our rainfall scatterplot: it would be a confused mess!). Just like clustered bar charts or box plots they can show more than one variable in order to make comparisons.

Figure 8 shows the number of men (blue) and women (red) enrolled on masters and doctoral programmes in the USA. Women have outnumbered men on masters courses for 30 years, but only just over 10 years ago did they start to outnumber men on doctoral programmes.

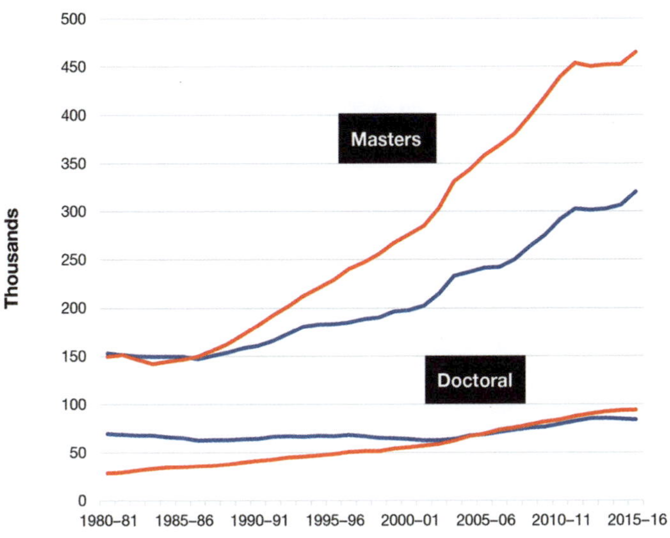

Figure 8 Enrollment on US masters and doctoral programmes, 1980–2016

CHECKPOINT

Using the three questions to understand a line graph

Examine Figure 8 and ask our three questions.

1 What is displayed on each axis?

Vertical axis: ....

Horizontal axis: ....

2 Does each axis show continuous variation or categories?

Vertical: ....

Horizontal: ....

3 Does the graph show original data or summaries of it?

....

Answers

1 Vertical axis: number of students
Horizontal axis: years
2 Vertical: continuous variation
Horizontal: continuous variation
3 Original data

DO IT YOURSELF

HOW TO INTERPRET GRAPHS

Look back at the graphs in this section and consider the questions you answered about them. Then use those answers to help you interpret the data the graphs communicate.

1 Using Figure 4:

In which ethnic group was support for Clinton strongest?

....

In which ethnic group(s) was support for Trump higher than for Clinton?

....

2 Using Figure 6:

In which country do men and women have the most similar weekly working hours?

Compare interquartile range and the medians

....

3 Using Figure 7:

How many inches of rain should one expect in a usual UK winter?

....

4 Using Figure 8:

How many students altogether were enrolled in either masters or doctoral programmes?

In 1980

....

In 2015

....

Answers

1 Black
White

2 Switzerland, UK, Sweden

3 between 150 and 300 inches.

4 about 400,000
about 1,000,000

Section

Expressing very small or large numbers

What is scientific notation?

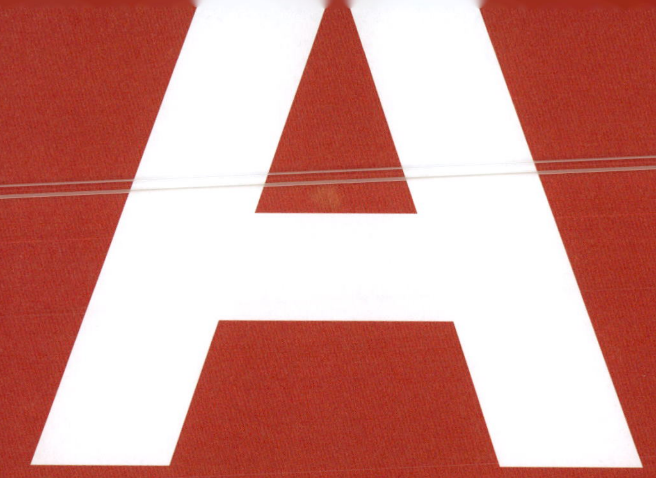

To save writing tedious lists of zeroes, we use *scientific notation* for very large or very small numbers.

Scientific notation eliminates hassle

Our number system is based on ten. A power of ten is the number ten multiplied by itself that number of times, or the number one with that number of zeroes after it.

Scientific notation uses powers of ten to rewrite any number as a number *between* one and ten multiplied by a *power of ten*. It allows us to represent very big or very small numbers without having to write a lot of zeroes.

INTERPRETING VERY LARGE AND VERY SMALL NUMBERS

Using numbers to convey very large or small amounts is often cumbersome.

There are about 7 billion billion billion atoms in the average human body. That is 7,000,000,000,000,000,000,000,000,000 atoms.

The mass of an electron is about 0.0000000000000000000000000009 grams.

It is very hard to imagine either number. It is just as tedious to write them out as it is to count all those zeroes. Instead we use scientific notation.

A NUMBER SYSTEM BASED ON TEN

We base our number system on the number ten and so we write down numbers, reading from right to left, in units, tens of units, ten times tens of units (hundreds), ten times ten times tens of units (thousands), and so on. For example

$$\begin{aligned} 5243 &= 5000 + 200 + 40 + 3 \\ &= 5 \times (10 \times 10 \times 10) + 2 \times (10 \times 10) + 4 \times 10 + 3 \times 1 \end{aligned}$$

As we move farther to the left in a number each digit represents a ten-fold increase in the units we are dealing with.

THE 'POWER' OF TEN

Instead of repeating 'ten times ten times ten...' we can use the concept of *power* as a shorthand. **The power of a number is the number of times we multiply it by *itself*.** Thus 'ten to the power two', written as 10^2, is ten multiplied by ten, 10^3 is ten multiplied by ten multiplied by ten, and so on. 10^1 is just the number ten by itself, and $10^0 = 1$.

$10^1 = 10$

$10^2 = 10 \times 10 = 100$

$10^3 = 10 \times 10 \times 10 = 1000$

$10^4 = 10 \times 10 \times 10 \times 10 = 10{,}000$

TWO RULES OF POWER

1. The power is the same as the number of zeroes in each number above.

2. The number expressed by each power also corresponds to each column of our number system as we move leftwards. These are just two different ways of saying exactly the same thing.

$$5243 = 5000 + 200 + 40 + 3$$
$$= 5 \times 1000 + 2 \times 100 + 4 \times 10 + 3 \times 1$$
$$5243 = 5 \times 10^3 + 2 \times 10^2 + 4 \times 10^1 + 3 \times 10^0$$

USING POWER TO REPRESENT LARGE AND SMALL NUMBERS

We can use the powers of ten to represent any number, no matter how big or small, in only a few digits. We use a number greater than one and less than ten and then multiply it by a power of ten. The total number of zeroes *or* other numbers counted after the first digit in any number then get converted into a power of ten. This is called *scientific notation.*

30 = 3 followed by one digit = 3×10^1

$795{,}000$ = 7 followed by 5 digits = 7.95×10^5

The number of atoms in the human body can now be written as 7×10^{27}.

Small numbers can be dealt with in exactly the same way. Negative powers are equal to the number one *divided by* the corresponding positive power of ten.

Now the number of the power gives the number of digits *after* the decimal point.

The mass of an electron becomes about 9×10^{-28} grams.

In scientific notation capital letter **E is often used to stand for '10 raised to the power of'.**

$$4.82 \times 10^{2} = 4.82E2$$

$$2.893257 \times 10^{6} = 2.893257E6$$

$$3.2 \times 10^{-4} = 3.2E\text{-}4$$

WHAT DOES 'E' IN THE MIDDLE OF A NUMBER MEAN?

CHECKPOINT

Writing in scientific notation

Write the following numbers using scientific notation

1 37,000,000,000,000 = ...

2 0.000342 = ...

3 7,835,600 = ...

Answers

1 3.7E13

2 3.42E-4

3 7.8356E6

Section 7

Seven simple rules

How can I use and interpret numbers in data well?

There are seven simple rules to follow when using or interpreting numerical data.

Seven simple rules to number success

Numerical data is an essential way to present clear and concise evidence for any argument. Be sceptical of arguments made without numbers! However, numbers can be used well or badly. Following the seven rules set out in this section will help you avoid some common problems and interpret numbers with confidence and clarity.

Never use a number if you don't know where it has been

Numbers are only as good as the process that produces them. **Any number depends upon a clear definition of *what* is measured and *how* it is measured.** Very often it is difficult or impossible to measure precisely what is actually wanted (to obtain a *valid* measurement) in a way that will give consistent results whenever it is repeated (*reliable* measurements).

Numbers are more robust if they are based on definitions and measurements that are widely agreed, and whose strengths and weaknesses are well understood. Always give the source of numbers you use, and be suspicious of numerical evidence presented without a source.

2 Comparisons need care

Comparisons over time or across different groups can only be made if the measurement method stays the same, which is often difficult to ensure. Definitions used by different organizations or countries or in different time periods rarely coincide exactly.

3 Embrace uncertainty

Often it is sensible to report a range within which the true value of a measurement is thought to lie. ‘Around half’ or ‘48 to 52%’ is better than ‘50.00%’ when **we are not certain of the accuracy of the data being used**.

However, number ranges that do not have *both* upper *and* lower limits are meaningless. ‘Up to 99% of people’ includes the number zero; ‘as few as 1%’ does not rule out 99%. My local supermarket sells a cleaning product that boasts that it removes ‘up to 100% of grease and dirt’. Even if it had no effect at all, that claim would be true!

Orders of magnitude matter

It is easy to misplace a decimal point or confuse a million with a billion, and thus get a number wildly wrong. **Numbers should be presented with some readily recognizable comparisons that make their magnitude comprehensible.** This also makes the detection of any errors more likely.

5 Avoid making mountains out of molehills

A sense of perspective is always important. It is often tempting to assume that *any* difference we find in two numbers or two results in some data *must* be important, no matter how small. Outside of subatomic physics, this is rarely the case, if only because **almost all data comes with a margin of error**. As a *very* rough rule of thumb, I would want to see one number 10% larger or smaller than another before I paid attention to the difference.

(At least) two is company

A number presented on its own may be there just to give a spurious air of scientific credibility to an argument. Usually **we need to make *comparisons* between numbers to make sense of what is going on.** Graphs are useful precisely because they highlight such comparisons.

7 Three is plenty

It is easy to get carried away with numbers; however, your **readers will soon switch off if you use too many**. There are two remedies for this

- Round numbers to three significant digits or less to avoid long lists of figures

- Use a picture to tell the story: the charts we examined here all present a large volume of numbers intuitively using colour, shape and space; they are much easier on readers' eyes than the raw figures behind them.

CHECKPOINT

Which of the following should you do when using numerical data?

1 Only use a number that has a clear definition of what it measures and how it measures.

2 Only make comparisons across groups where the measurement method is the same.

3 Understand that you cannot be absolutely certain of the accuracy of the data.

4 Present a number with an easily recognizable comparison.

5 Do not assume all differences between numbers are important.

6 Present enough numbers to make comparisons, but do not use too many at once.

All of the above!

CONGRATULATIONS!
My confidence in using and interpreting numbers is now
/ 10!
#LittleQuickFix

Work through this checklist to help ensure you have mastered all you need to know

- ☐ Do you know why we need numbers? If not, go back to page 13.
- ☐ Do you understand the two key differences between the mean and the median? If not, go back to page 23.
- ☐ Do you know how to measure and calculate the spread of data? If not, go back to page 37.
- ☐ Do you remember the three questions you can use to decipher any graph? If not, go back to page 62.

HOW TO KNOW YOU ARE DONE

- ☐ Are you able to distinguish the five most common types of graphs? If not, go back to page 72.
- ☐ Do you know how to interpret the five most common types of graphs? If not, go back to page 74.
- ☐ Are you confident in writing numbers in scientific notation? If not, go back to page 103.
- ☐ Can you list the seven rules to follow for using and interpreting numbers well? If not, go back to page 118.

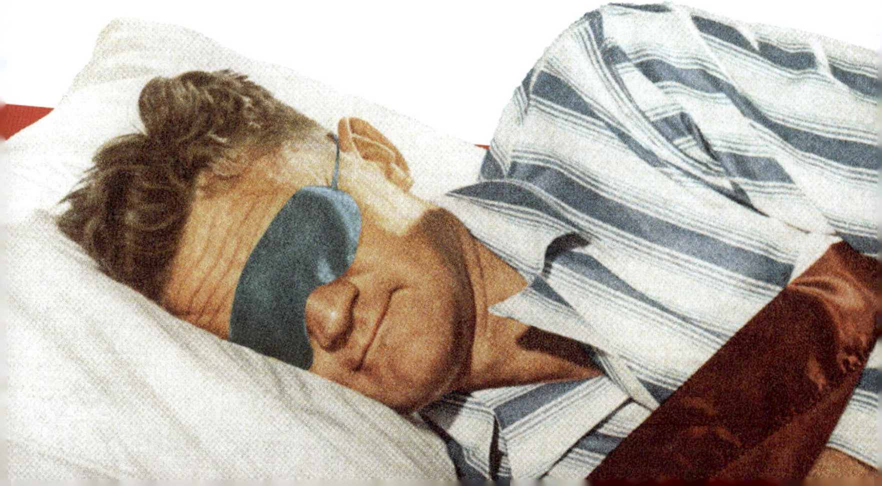

Glossary

Average The typical, usual or central value in a series of numerical data. See *mean* and *median.*

Bar chart A chart in which the length or height of a bar corresponds to the number or proportions in a data series.

Box plot A chart in which a box corresponds to the quartiles in a data series with a whisker extending to the outliers for that data.

Central tendency An alternative term for *average* or *level.*

Continuous value range A range of values expressed directly in meaningful numbers (e.g. income in $; height in cm; temperature in degrees Celsius).

Coordinate A data point on a scatterplot or line graph, depicting the value for that case on each of the two axes.

Dispersion An alternative term for *spread.*

Histogram A chart in which the area of the chart above any range of values corresponds to the proportion of observations with those values.

Horizontal axis The axis of any chart that lies horizontally, with numbers going from left to right.

Interquartile range The *upper quartile* minus the *lower quartile*; a measure of the spread of data.

Level The typical, usual or central value for a series of data.

Line graph A scatterplot in which a series of data points are joined by a line.

Lower quartile The coordinates one-quarter of the way up a ranked series of data.

Mean The arithmetic average of a data series, calculated by summing the values of all the observations and dividing by the total number of observations.

Median The value exactly halfway up a ranked data series, or the average of the two central values if the data series has an even number of observations.

Outlier A value lying far above or below other values in a series.

Power The number of times a number is multiplied by itself (e.g. $10^3 = 10 \times 10 \times 10$).

Residual The value found by subtracting the mean of all observations from the value for an observation.

Scatterplot A chart in which two series of data for the same set of cases is presented, plotted against each of the two axes.

Scientific notation Numbers presented as a number between 1 and 10, multiplied by power of 10.

Spread The distribution of data around its mean. The greater the average absolute distance of observations to the mean, the greater the dispersion or spread.

Square root The square root of any number is the number that, multiplied by itself, produces the original number (e.g. the square root of 9 is 3 since $3 \times 3 = 9$).

Squared residual The square of the distance between a value in a data series and the mean value.

Standard deviation A measure of spread based on squared residuals.

Vertical axis The axis of any chart that lies vertically to the left of the chart, with numbers going from the bottom to the top.